What's for lunch?

Potatoes

Library of Congress Cataloging-in-Publication Data
Llewellyn, Claire.
    Potatoes / Claire Llewellyn.
    p.   cm -- (What's For Lunch?)
    Includes Index.
    Summary: Presents facts about the potato, including where
    and how it is grown, harvested, and marketed,
    and what other products are made from potatoes.
    ISBN 0-516-20838-1
    1. Potatoes--Juvenile literature.   2. Potato products--Juvenile
literature.   [1. Potatoes. 2. Potato products.] I. Title II. Series.
Llewellyn, Claire. What's for Lunch?
SB211.P8L55 1998   97-34924
641.3'521--dc21   CIP
                                           AC

First American edition 1998 by
Franklin Watts
A Divison of Grolier Publishing
Sherman Turnpike
Danbury
CT, 06816

ISBN 0-516-20838-1

Editor: Samantha Armstrong
Series Designer: Kirstie Billingham
Designer: Kelly Flynn
Consultant: The Potato Marketing Board
Reading Consultant: Prue Goodwin, Reading and Language
Information Centre, Reading.

Printed in Hong Kong

What's for lunch?

Potatoes

Claire Llewellyn

CHILDREN'S PRESS®

A Division of Grolier Publishing

NEW YORK • LONDON • HONG KONG • SYDNEY
DANBURY, CONNECTICUT

Today we are having potatoes for lunch.
Potatoes are a **vegetable**.
They contain **vitamins**, **fiber**, and **starch**.
They give us **energy**.

Potatoes are grown all over the world.
There are many different kinds of potatoes.

They can be large or small, and
red, brown, or white.

Potatoes grow on plants.
Most plants grow from
a seed, but potato plants
grow from another potato.
In spring, farmers plant
rows and rows of potatoes.

On every potato
there are little marks called **eyes**.
When the potato is planted,
shoots grow from the eyes.

After a few weeks, one of the shoots
grows toward the light
and bursts through the soil.
Under the ground,
the plant is growing **roots** and **stems**.

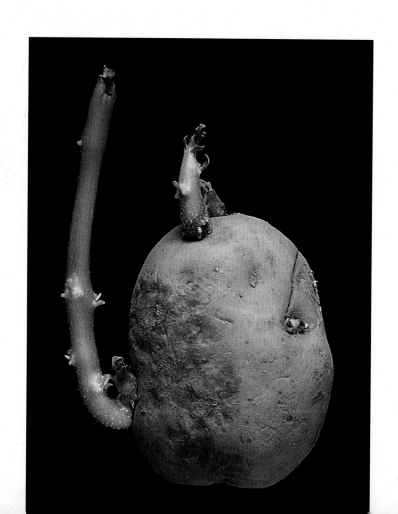

The fields are soon full of low,
bushy potato plants.
Meanwhile, under the ground tiny
swellings called **tubers** grow on the stems.
These become the potatoes that we eat.

Farmers water the plants
and spray them with **chemicals**
to protect them from
pests and disease.
The potatoes grow underground,
in the dark.
If any light gets on
the potatoes, they will
turn green and
be bad to eat.

In autumn, the leaves on the plants **wither**.
Under the ground, the potatoes
are ready for **harvesting**.
A **potato harvester** digs up the potatoes
and shakes off the stones and soil as well.

The potatoes are packed into sacks
and stored in a cool, dark place.
Some are saved for planting next spring.

Most of the potatoes are sold to stores, markets, and supermarkets, where you can buy them to cook at home.
Others are sold to restaurants and hotels.

The potatoes are washed and sorted
into different sizes before they are eaten.
Any damaged or green ones are removed.

Potatoes are used in many different ways.
Some are made into potato chips.
Different flavorings are added
to give them special tastes.

Potatoes can be sliced up
and fried to make french fries.
Potatoes contain a lot of **starch**.
Starch is smooth and sticky
and is used in ice cream.

Potatoes are eaten
all over the world
in all kinds of ways.

They can be dipped
into sauces,
eaten with curry,
and made into croquettes.
Potatoes are filling and good for you.

29

Glossary

chemical	something that farmers use on their plants to keep them healthy and strong
disease	something that attacks plants
energy	the strength to work and play
eyes	the parts of a potato from which the shoots grow
fiber	something found in certain foods that helps us to digest the food we eat
pest	an insect that attacks plants
potato harvester	a machine that pulls up the potato plant and shakes off the soil
roots	the part of a plant that grows underground and takes moisture and goodness from the soil

seed   the part of a plant that grows into a new plant

starch   a smooth, sticky substance found in potatoes. It is used in ice cream.

stem   the underground part of the potato plant that the tubers grow on

tuber   a growth on an underground stem that swells into a vegetable

vegetable   a plant grown for the parts that can be eaten

vitamin   something that is found in fresh fruit and vegetables that keeps the body healthy

wither   shrivel up—leaves on a plant do this when the growing season is over

Index

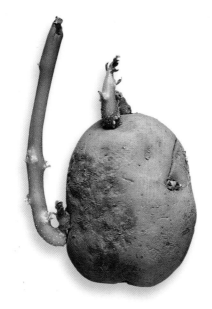

Picture credits: Barrie Watts 12, 13, 15, 18; Holt Studios International 9, 14, 16, 17, 19 (all Nigel Cattlin), 20, 21, 23 (all Richard Anthony); Reed Farmers Publishing Picture Library 10-11; Tayto Ltd. 25; Zefa 22; Steve Shott cover; All other photographs Tim Ridley, Wells Street Studios, London.
With thanks to Redmond and Roxanne Carney.